Contents

Childhood

Isambard Kingdom Brunel was born on 9 April 1806 in Portsmouth. His father, Marc Brunel, was an engineer. An engineer plans and makes all kinds of machines and buildings.

Marc Brunel was French and had spent six years in the French Navy making maps. Then there was a revolution in France and the King was killed. Marc had supported the King and had to escape to America. He became the chief engineer of New York, planning the city's buildings. Later he settled in Britain, where he married Sophia Kingdom.

Marc's ideas made him famous. He designed knitting and boot-making machines, a sawmill to cut and shape timber, and engines for steam-powered riverboats.

The British Navy needed parts for its sailing ships. Marc designed special machines to make these parts.

Isambard's father,
Marc Brunel

Famous People

Isambard Kingdom Brunel

1806 – 1859

Martin Malcolm

Martin Malcolm is a writer, teacher and storyteller. His other books for 4Learning include *Poetry By Numbers*, *Animated Tales of the World* and *A Giant in Ancient Egypt*.

Published by 4Learning
124 Horseferry Road
London
SW1P 2TX
Tel: 08701 246 444
www.channel4.com/learning

Author: Martin Malcolm
Education Officer: Anne Fleck
Editor: Jackie Mace
Illustrator: Gary Wing
Picture Researcher: Sam Munday
Designer: Periscope Design Solutions
Printer: ESP Colour
Project Manager: Huw Jones
ISBN 18621 5984 X

At the dockyards, young Isambard saw his
father's machines at work. He was fascinated.
Later, he saw the wagons that ran along iron
rails bringing timber into his father's sawmill.
Isambard began to dream about the things
he would build one day. He would be just like
his famous father. He would be the greatest
engineer in the world.

Growing up

When he was four, Isambard was already drawing buildings and machines. By the time he was six, he was learning to do complicated maths. Marc Brunel was very proud of his son and taught him as much as he could.

As he grew older, Isambard went rowing on the river and made model boats. He was a very good swimmer and could hold his breath under water for a long time. He was a daring boy who loved climbing the high garden wall and balancing on the top. He seemed to have no fear of heights.

You've got great talent. You'll go far.

When Isambard was sent to boarding school in Hove, he spent his spare time drawing all the important buildings in the town. He called these sketches his surveys. Engineers like his father made surveys, so Isambard did the same. One day, Isambard told his friends and teachers that a new building near the school was unsafe. Nobody believed him – how could a 13-year-old boy know more about buildings than the grown-ups who designed and built them? The following day, there was a rumble and the building came crashing down. Isambard had been right!

Apprentice engineer

When he was 14, Isambard was sent to Paris to learn more about mathematics. He went on to work for Louis Breguet, the most famous watchmaker in the world. Isambard loved the complicated levers and cogs in the watches and learned to make them.

By 1823, Isambard was back in England and working as his father's assistant. He spent a lot of time in the workshops of Henry Maudslay. Maudslay had built many of Marc's inventions and showed Isambard how to use engineering tools.

Isambard's mind was busy with dreams of the great things he would do. He called these dreams his 'castles in Spain' and wondered if they would ever come true.

Things were not going well for Marc Brunel. His sawmill was nearly destroyed by fire and he had lost a

Isambard learned to make watches like this one.

lot of money. In 1821 he even spent time in prison because he couldn't pay his bills.

Then, Marc and Isambard were asked to build something that had never been done before – a tunnel underneath a huge river! It was to go under the River Thames in London. But could such a daring idea be made to work? In 1825 there were no bulldozers or earth-moving machines. Everything would have to be done by hand.

The tunnel under the River Thames would need to be 375 metres long.

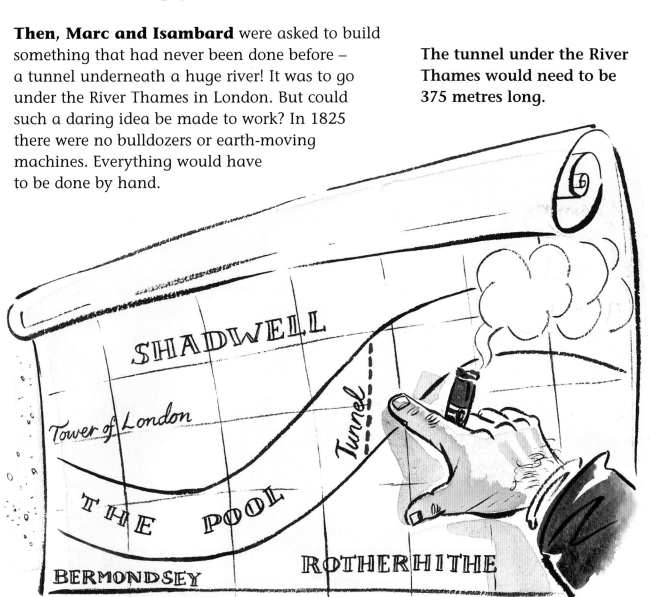

SHADWELL

Tower of London

Tunnel

THE POOL

BERMONDSEY

ROTHERHITHE

Adventures underground

To make the **Thames Tunnel**, a huge brick tower was built on the riverbank. Workers dug out the ground under the tower so that it began to sink. After weeks of hard digging, the whole tower had been sunk into the ground to make a waterproof shaft. From the bottom of this shaft, the workers began digging a tunnel underneath the river.

Marc Brunel designed a shield to hold up the walls of the tunnel so the workers could dig out 15 centimetres of mud at a time. It was dangerous work. Many workers caught diseases. Marc became very ill, leaving 20-year-old Isambard in charge.

The tunnelling shield was big enough to hold 36 workers.

Isambard worked in the tunnel for days at a time. Then disaster struck – the roof collapsed and the tunnel filled with water! Workers scrambled out, but one man was trapped. Isambard went back into the rising water and dragged him to safety.

Using a diving bell, Isambard found a hole in the riverbed. He even put one foot through the hole and onto the top of the tunnelling shield. The hole was filled in with bags of clay and digging began again. Isambard held a party in the tunnel to celebrate, with fine food and a military band.

Eight months later there was a second tunnel collapse. Six men were killed and Isambard nearly drowned. He was ill for many months and never worked in the tunnel again.

Marc Brunel did not give up.
Seventeen years later he completed the tunnel. Marc proudly carried his three-year-old grandson through it – the first person to cross the Thames by land!

Isambard used a diving bell to explore damage to the tunnel.

Adventures overground

In **1833, Isambard** was asked to build a 180-kilometre railway between Bristol and London. Railways were still a new idea and nothing as long as this had ever been built before. Night and day, Isambard rode backwards and forwards between Bristol and London planning the route. It took until 1841 for the railway to be completed. Isambard chose Daniel Gooch to build the steam locomotives.

Firefly, **designed by Daniel Gooch**

Isambard's railway tracks were wider than those in the rest of England. The distance between the rails is called the gauge and Isambard thought this broad gauge would make the ride smoother and faster. The different-sized tracks made journeys between Isambard's railway (called the Great Western Railway) and other railways difficult. However fifty years later, the Great Western's railway tracks were changed to match those in the rest of England. Many people said the broad gauge had been a costly mistake.

There will never be any progress if we do not try new things!

A racing steam engine in action

Isambard called his railway 'the finest work in England', but it had been very hard to build. A two-mile tunnel under Box Hill, near the city of Bath, had taken nearly five years of work and at least 100 men died building it. Isambard went on to plan railways in Devon, Cornwall, Italy and Eastern Bengal.

In Devon, he experimented with a new way of making the trains run, using pumps to suck the carriages along the track. However, this atmospheric railway could not be made to work properly. After losing a lot of money, it was scrapped and steam locomotives had to be used instead.

The Royal Albert Bridge

The Royal Albert Bridge between Devon and Cornwall. Isambard designed this bridge for his trains to cross a river 339 metres wide and 22 metres deep.

Adventures with bridges

When he first came to Bristol, Isambard designed a bridge over the Avon Gorge. It was a suspension bridge – one that would hang from chains over the enormous gap. To start the work, an iron bar 300 metres long was pushed across the gorge at a place called Clifton. A basket was hung from ropes underneath so workers could be pulled from one side to the other. Isambard was the first to try it. Halfway across, the basket got stuck. Isambard climbed out and freed the ropes, hanging 66 metres above the ground!

The Clifton Suspension Bridge ran out of money and was not finished in Isambard's lifetime, but he built many other great bridges, such as the one at Maidenhead, which can still be seen today.

I'll lead my workers by example!

16

The Royal Albert Bridge is still in use today.

Isambard also built the Royal Albert Bridge over the River Tamar between Devon and Cornwall. To make the central pier – the support post in the middle of the river – was the biggest problem. He designed a huge iron tube. This was floated into the middle of the river, tipped up and sunk until one end reached the riverbed. Then, the water was pumped out and bricks were built up inside the tube. Isambard had remembered his father's idea for the Thames Tunnel and used it in a new way.

Long iron bars called girders were floated out and fixed to the pier to make the bridge. Isambard gave orders to his men from high up on the pier, using flags as signals. Hundreds of people came to watch.

Adventures at sea

Isambard wanted his Great Western Railway to take people further. 'Why not build a steamship to carry passengers between Bristol and New York?' he asked. People laughed. Sailing ships went to New York, but steam had only ever been used to power small riverboats. No one believed the idea could work. Isambard proved them wrong.

Great Western on her maiden voyage to New York

The first ship he designed was made of wood and called *Great Western*. As well as sails, there were two steam-powered paddle wheels on the sides of the ship. On a test run, the funnel of the ship caught fire and Isambard was badly hurt. But when *Great Western* finally took to the seas, she crossed from England to New York in just 15 days – much faster than any other ship.

Great Eastern was a giant iron ship – the biggest the world had ever seen. It was very hard to launch such a big ship. There was an accident and one man died. Bad luck seemed to follow the ship. On her first journey, Isambard had a heart attack. The struggle to build *Great Eastern* had brought him close to death. A week later, a funnel exploded and five men were killed. Isambard was deeply shocked. He never recovered.

Great Britain being repaired in Dundrum Bay, northern Ireland

Next, Isambard built *Great Britain*. She was made out of iron and was much stronger. Instead of paddle wheels, there was a screw propeller. This meant she could travel much faster. In 1846, *Great Britain* was wrecked on rocks off the Irish coast. She was so strong that she did not break up. She was repaired and re-floated. *Great Britain* is now moored in Bristol as a floating museum.

Isambard Kingdom Brunel at the launch of *Great Eastern*

Family life

Isambard and his wife, Mary, had three children called Isambard, Henry and Florence. Isambard enjoyed making his children laugh with magic tricks. Once, when doing a trick, he accidentally swallowed a gold coin. He designed a special table that doctors used to swing his body around and get the coin out.

Isambard entertained his family with magic tricks.

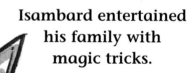

Isambard was so busy that he did not have much time for his family. In his diary, he wrote that he felt as if he was married to his work! He dreamed of retiring and planned a grand country house to live in.

Isambard bought some land at Watcomb Park in Devon for his great house. Sadly, he never had the chance to build it. He had an illness called Bright's disease and the long, hard work of building his last ship, *Great Eastern,* tired him out. He knew that he would soon die.

In 1859 his Royal Albert Bridge was opened. Isambard could no longer walk, but was laid on a wagon and gently pulled across the bridge, so he could take a last look at his masterpiece. He died on 15 September 1859. He was just 53 years old.

The last photograph of Isambard was taken on the deck of *Great Eastern*.

The world's greatest engineer?

In 1827, at the age of 21, Isambard had written a note to himself in his diary:

'Be the first engineer and an example for all future ones.'

He was always keen to try out new ideas. When he was told that soldiers were dying in the Crimean War because the hospitals were unclean, he designed a new kind of hospital. It was built in just two months and could be kept much cleaner. Many soldiers lived as a result of the germ-free conditions.

The Clifton Suspension Bridge as it appears today

After his death, Isambard's Clifton Suspension Bridge was finished by other engineers. It stands now as a reminder of him.

This statue of Isambard Kingdom Brunel stands in London's Paddington Station to remind people about his work.

The railways, bridges and steamships engineered by Isambard showed that things that were once thought impossible could really be done. While some people say that many of his projects were disasters that cost money and lives, others say that he was the world's greatest engineer.

What do you think?

Isambard was brave and determined. Many of the things he built are still around today.

He spent his life solving problems and finding ways to make people's lives better.

He was only interested in glory. Men died as a result of his grand plans.

He just wouldn't listen. His mistakes on the railways cost a lot of money.

He inspired other engineers to think of wonderful new buildings and machines.

A timeline of Brunel's life

Events in Isambard Kingdom Brunel's life

Isambard Kingdom Brunel was born

Thames Tunnel was started

Foundation stone for the Clifton Suspension Bridge was laid

1803	1806	1815	1825	1833	1836	1837

Events in the world

Richard Trevithick built the first steam locomotive

Battle of Waterloo ended the war between Britain and France

Factory Act stopped children under 9 years of age from working in factories

Victoria became Queen

First
voyage
of the
steamship
*Great
Western*

Thames
Tunnel
was
completed

Shipwreck
of
*Great
Britain*

Royal
Albert
Bridge
was
opened
and
Isambard
Kingdom
Brunel
died

The
steamship
*Great
Eastern*
was
built

Clifton
Suspension
Bridge
finally
opened

1838 1842 1846 1851 1854 1858 1859 1864

Queen
Victoria's
first
railway
trip

The
Great
Exhibition
took place

Crimean
war
started

Charles
Darwin
published
his
theory
of
evolution,
*On the
Origin of
Species*

Geneva
Convention
signed,
giving
rights to
soldiers at
war

Glossary

Turn to the page number in brackets to see how each word is used in the text.

design *(4)* To plan or sketch something, such as a building or machine.

diving bell *(11)* An open-bottomed container which can be used to explore deep water. Air is supplied by a tube to the person inside.

engineer *(4)* Someone whose job it is to plan and make all kinds of machines and buildings.

funnel *(18)* A chimney on a steamship or steam engine.

gauge *(12)* A measurement, such as the width between two rails on a railway line.

girder *(17)* A strong bar, usually made of iron.

gorge *(16)* A deep gap between two cliffs or hills.

iron *(5)* A metal used to make tools, rails, chains and machines. It can be shaped by heating or hammering.

locomotive *(12)* An engine which moves on wheels.

paddle wheels *(18)* Large wheels used to drive a ship through water.

pier *(17)* A support post for a bridge.

sawmill *(4)* A building with machinery for cutting and shaping wood.

screw propeller *(19)* A set of blades at the back of a ship which turn around to drive the ship through water.

survey *(7)* A careful plan, sketch or map of buildings or land, with measurements and notes.

suspension bridge *(16)* A bridge that hangs on chains rather than being held up by piers or posts.

timber *(4)* Trees or wood used for making buildings or ships.

How to find out more

More books to read

Brunel by Richard Tames
(Shire Publications, 2000)

Brunel and the Victorian Engineers by
Nigel Smith (Hodder Wayland, 1997)

Brunel: Historical Storybooks by Margaret
Nash and Jim Eldridge
(Hodder Wayland, 1998)

Brunel's Ships by Denis Griffiths,
Andrew Lambert and Fred Walker
(Chatham Publishing, 2000)

Famous Lives – Engineers by Peggy Burns
(Hodder Wayland, 1997)

Tell Me About Isambard Kingdom Brunel
by John Malam (Evans Brothers –
Books for Children, 1996)

The Usborne Book of Discovery by Struan
Reid and Patricia Fara (Usborne, 1994)

Places to visit

Brunel Atmospheric Railway Museum,
Starcross, Devon

Clifton Suspension Bridge Visitor
Centre, Bristol

National Maritime Museum, London

National Railway Museum, York

Railway Museum, Swindon

Royal Albert Bridge, Saltash

Science Museum, London

SS Great Britain, Bristol

Thames Tunnel Museum, Rotherhithe,
London

Index